Look-alike Animals

IS IT A BUTTERFLY OR A MOTH?

Susan B. Katz

a Capstone company — publishers for children

Raintree is an imprint of Capstone Global Library Limited, a company incorporated in England and Wales having its registered office at 264 Banbury Road, Oxford, OX2 7DY – Registered company number: 6695582

www.raintree.co.uk
myorders@raintree.co.uk

Hardback edition © Capstone Global Library Limited 2022
Paperback edition © Capstone Global Library Limited 2023
The moral rights of the proprietor have been asserted.

All rights reserved. No part of this publication may be reproduced in any form or by any means (including photocopying or storing it in any medium by electronic means and whether or not transiently or incidentally to some other use of this publication) without the written permission of the copyright owner, except in accordance with the provisions of the Copyright, Designs and Patents Act 1988 or under the terms of a licence issued by the Copyright Licensing Agency, 5th Floor, Shackleton House, 4 Battle Bridge Lane, London SE1 2HX (www.cla.co.uk). Applications for the copyright owner's written permission should be addressed to the publisher.

Edited by Christianne Jones
Designed by Elyse White
Original illustrations © Capstone Global Library Limited 2022
Picture research by Svetlana Zhurkin
Production by Laura Manthe
Originated by Capstone Global Library Ltd
Printed and bound in India

978 1 3982 2555 8 (hardback)
978 1 3982 2556 5 (paperback)

British Library Cataloguing in Publication Data
A full catalogue record for this book is available from the British Library.

Acknowledgements
We would like to thank the following for permission to reproduce photographs: Shutterstock: 22August, 18, Anna_Kova (design element), cover (middle) and throughout, Atosan, 26–27, BlueRingMedia, 20 (top), Breck P. Kent, 28–29 (top), Brett Hondow, 8, Carolyn Sebestyen, 29 (bottom), Cocos.Bounty, 11, Conrad Barrington, 22–23 (bottom), coxy58, 17, David James Chatterton, 16, davidtclay, 24, DM Meadows, 25 (bottom), ermess, 30, Florian Teodor, 21 (top), Ildiko Laskay, 12, Jay Ondreicka, 22–23 (top), josehidalgo87, 6, Jun Wat, cover (top), 13, Kirsanov Valeriy Vladimirovich, 15 (bottom), Kletr, 14–15, Landshark1, 25 (top), Muddy knees, 20 (bottom), Passakorn Umpornmaha, 19, Paul Reeves Photography, 7, Peter Etchells, 31, Ritam–Dmitrii Melgunov, 9, Rolf E. Staerk, 27 (bottom), Rudmer Zwerver, 3, Russell Marshall, 10, Sandra Standbridge, cover (bottom), Sari ONeal, 4, Simon Kovacic, 5, Tomar2, 28 (bottom), White Space Illustrations, 21 (bottom).

Every effort has been made to contact copyright holders of material reproduced in this book. Any omissions will be rectified in subsequent printings if notice is given to the publisher.

All the internet addresses (URLs) given in this book were valid at the time of going to press. However, due to the dynamic nature of the internet, some addresses may have changed, or sites may have changed or ceased to exist since publication. While the author and publisher regret any inconvenience this may cause readers, no responsibility for any such changes can be accepted by either the author or the publisher.

WHAT FLUTTERED BY?

Flitter, flutter!

A graceful, winged insect flits by. Was it a **butterfly** or a **moth?** Butterflies and moths are related. They look a lot alike. But they have some **differences.** Find out how you can tell these fancy flyers apart!

WING COLOURS

Look at those colourful wings!

Do you see **yellow, orange, blue, red** or other bright colours? It's likely that you're looking at a butterfly.

butterfly

Most moths have plain colours, such as white, beige or brown. A few types of moths are colourful, though.

moth

RESTING WINGS

All that flying can be tiring!

butterfly

When butterflies rest, they usually **close** their **wings**.

Moths often rest with their **wings open.** Some moths **overlap** their wings so they look like a tent. This hides their bodies. It helps keep them safe from animals that might eat them.

moth

WINGS TOGETHER OR APART?

Look very carefully!

Most moths have a hook-like part called a **frenulum** joining their front and hind wings together.

moth frenulum

Most butterflies do not have that, but there is one that does! It is the **regent skipper** butterfly in Australia.

butterfly

SIZE THEM UP!

Butterflies and moths come in all sizes.

Some have wingspans of less than **1.3 centimetres (0.5 inch)**.

Queen Alexandra's birdwing

The **Queen Alexandra's birdwing** is the largest butterfly in the world. It can have a wingspan of **30 centimetres (2 inches).**

Atlas moth

Hercules, Atlas and **white witch moths** are some of the largest moths. They have wingspans of **28 to 30 centimetres (11 to 12 inches).**

BODY PARTS

How many body parts can you see?

Butterflies and moths have three main parts. They are the **head, chest** and **abdomen.**

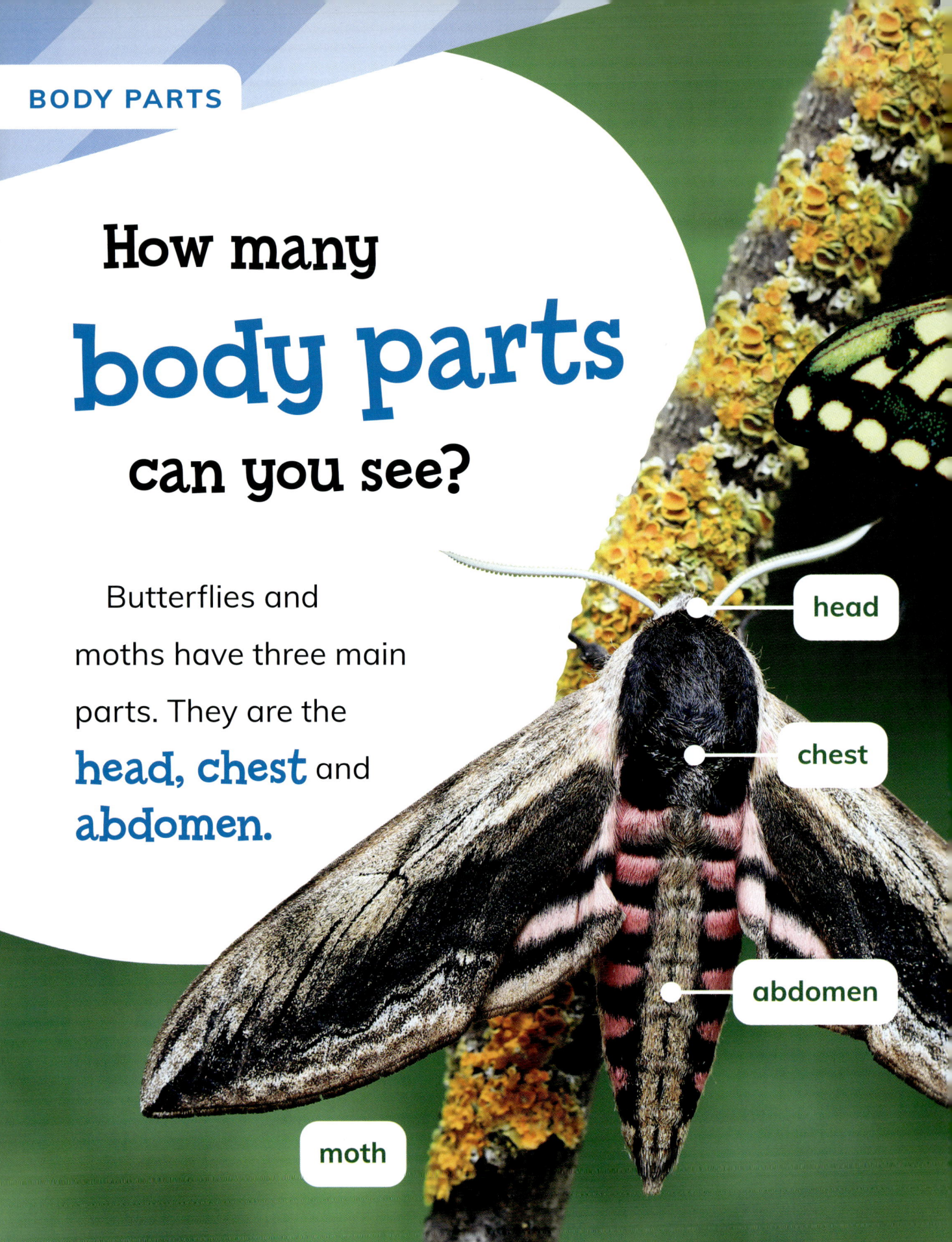

- head
- chest
- abdomen
- moth

Moths often have **wide, thick, hairy** bodies. Butterflies' bodies are usually **skinnier** and **smoother**. Both butterflies and moths also have **six legs** and **two antennae**.

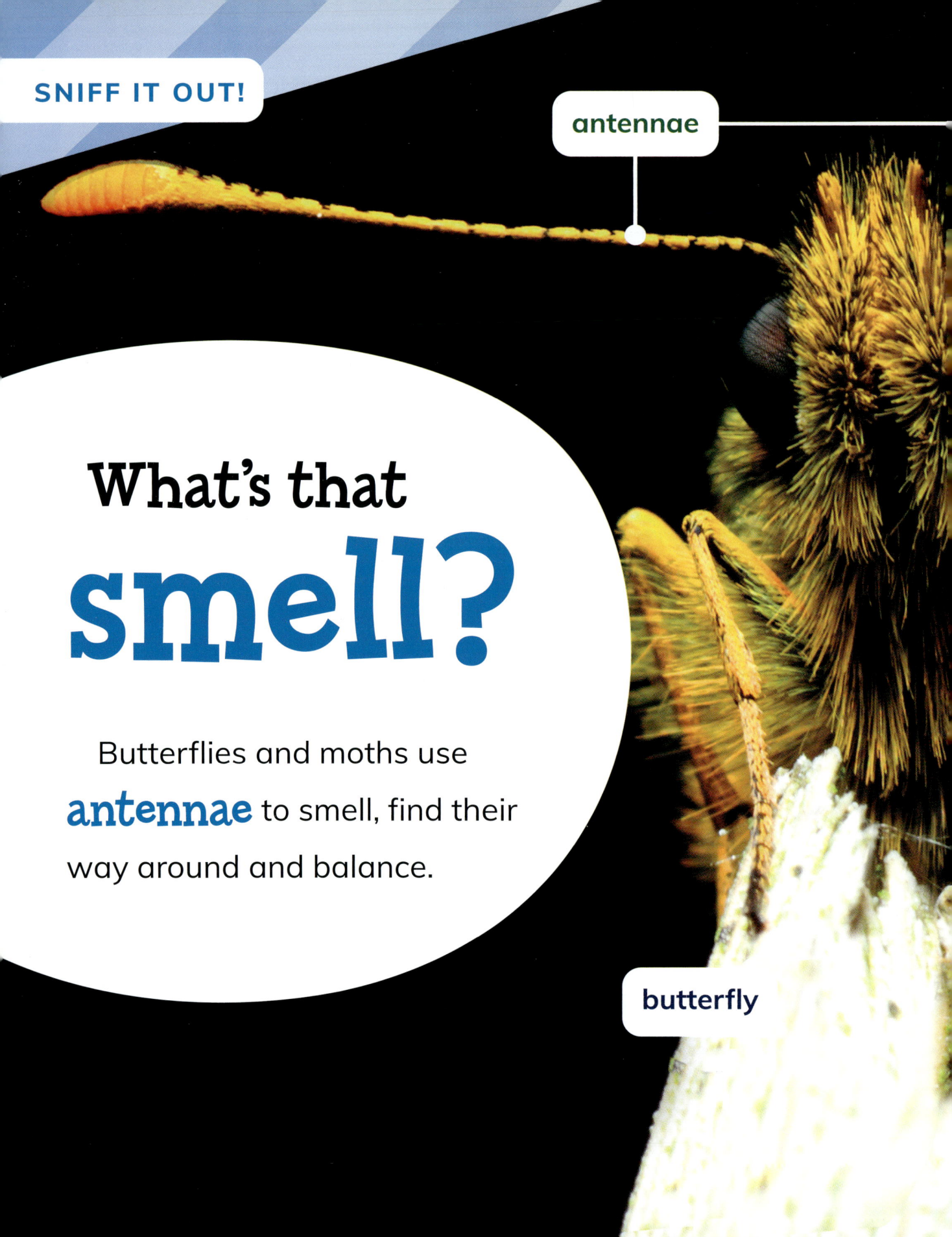

SNIFF IT OUT!

antennae

What's that smell?

Butterflies and moths use **antennae** to smell, find their way around and balance.

butterfly

Almost all butterflies have **long, thin antennae** that are club-shaped at the ends. Many moths have **feathery, short antennae.**

antennae

moth

SLURP IT UP!

butterfly

proboscis

Slurp! Slurp!

A butterfly or moth has a long straw-like **proboscis.** It helps them slurp up liquid. Butterflies and moths sip flower nectar, sap from trees and fruit juice.

proboscis

moth

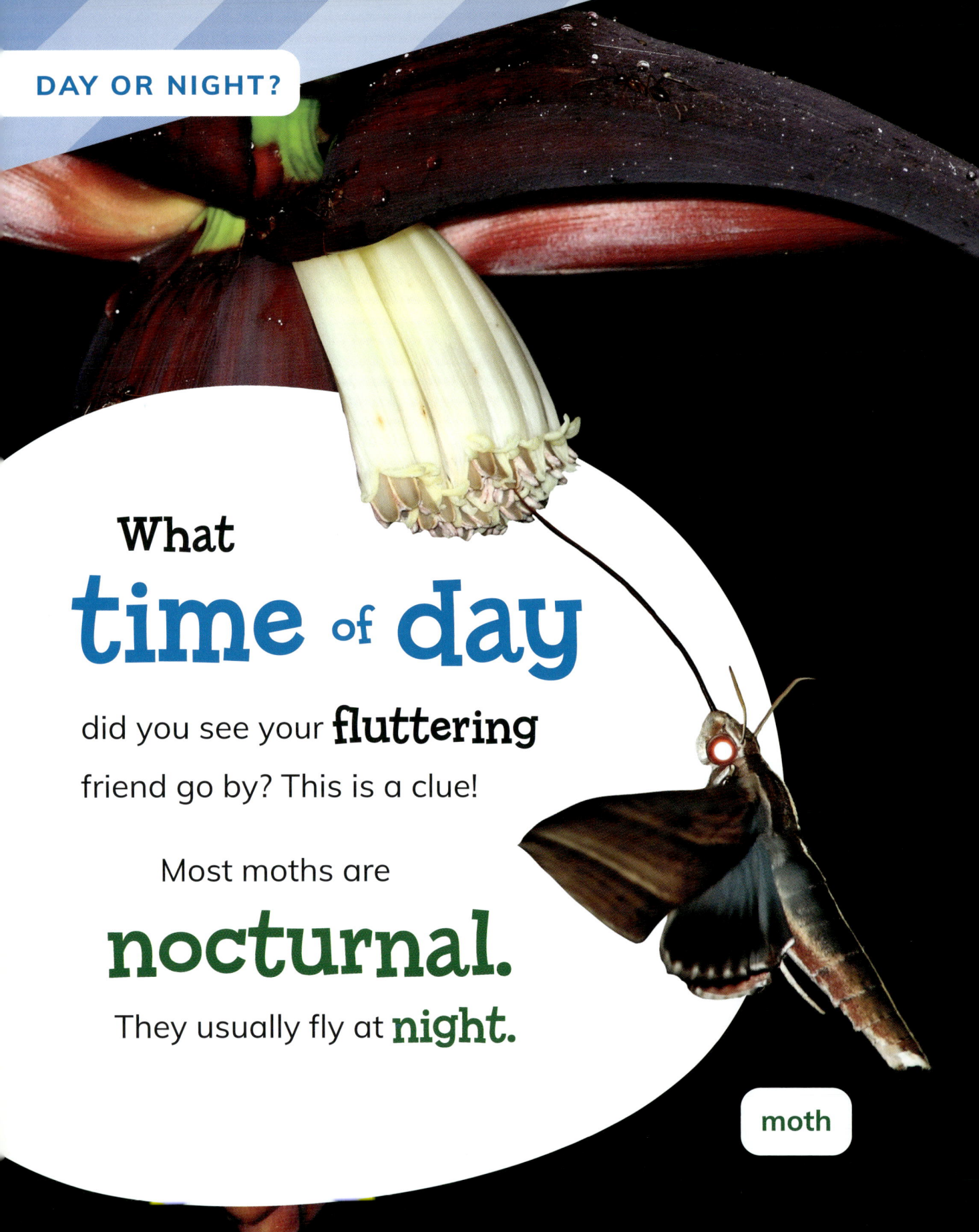

DAY OR NIGHT?

What **time of day** did you see your **fluttering** friend go by? This is a clue!

Most moths are **nocturnal.** They usually fly at **night.**

moth

butterfly

Most butterflies mainly flutter during the **daytime.** They are **diurnal.**

LIFE CYCLES

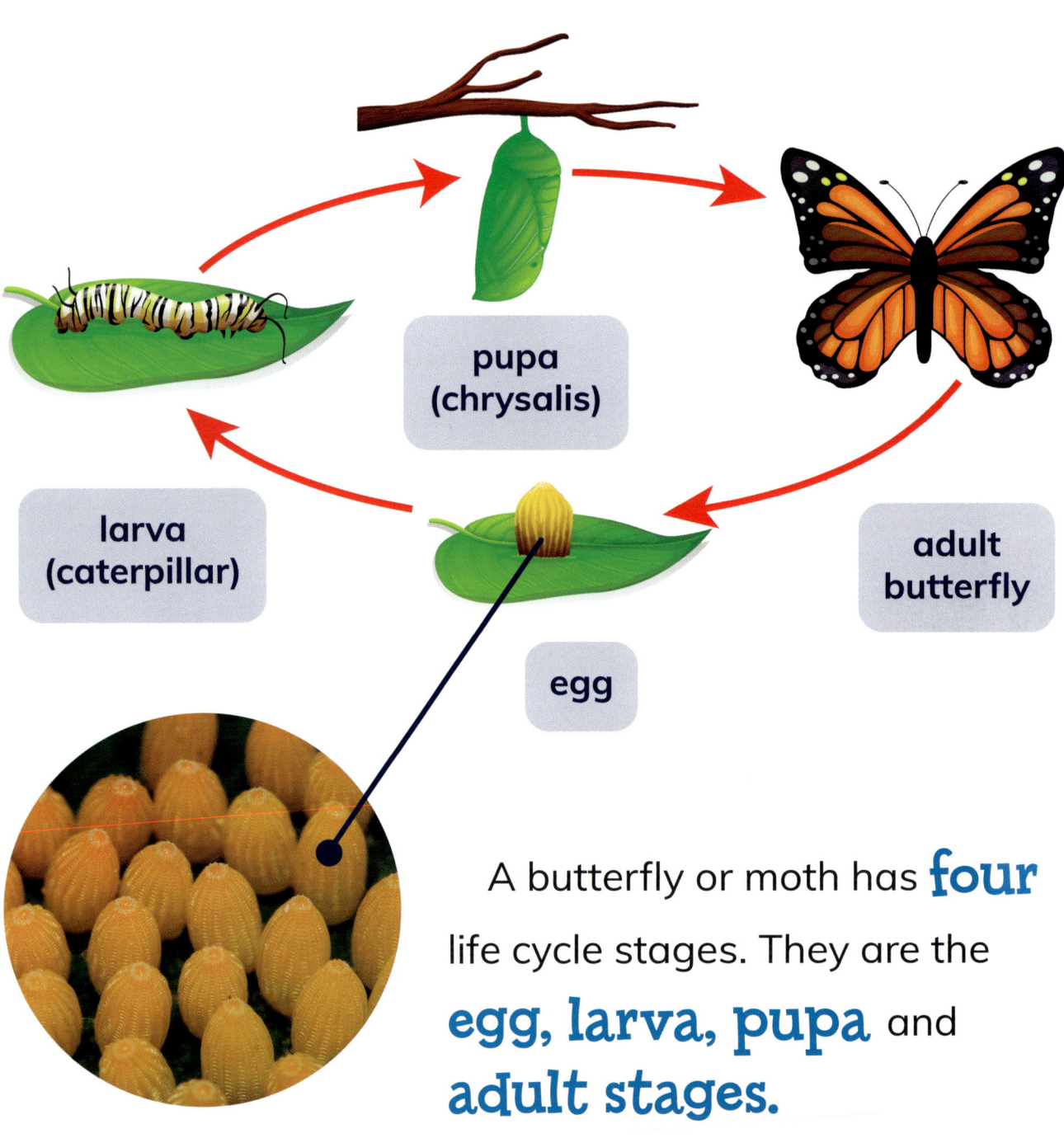

A butterfly or moth has **four** life cycle stages. They are the **egg, larva, pupa** and **adult stages.**

butterfly caterpillar

moth caterpillar

Caterpillars can be different colours or just one colour. They can be **furry** or **smooth.** Most furry caterpillars become moths.

BIG CHANGES

butterfly chrysalis

Time for big changes!

Metamorphosis happens when a caterpillar changes into a butterfly or moth. A moth changes inside a silky **cocoon.** A butterfly changes inside a shiny, smooth **chrysalis.** Butterflies and moths usually stay inside for 5 to 21 days.

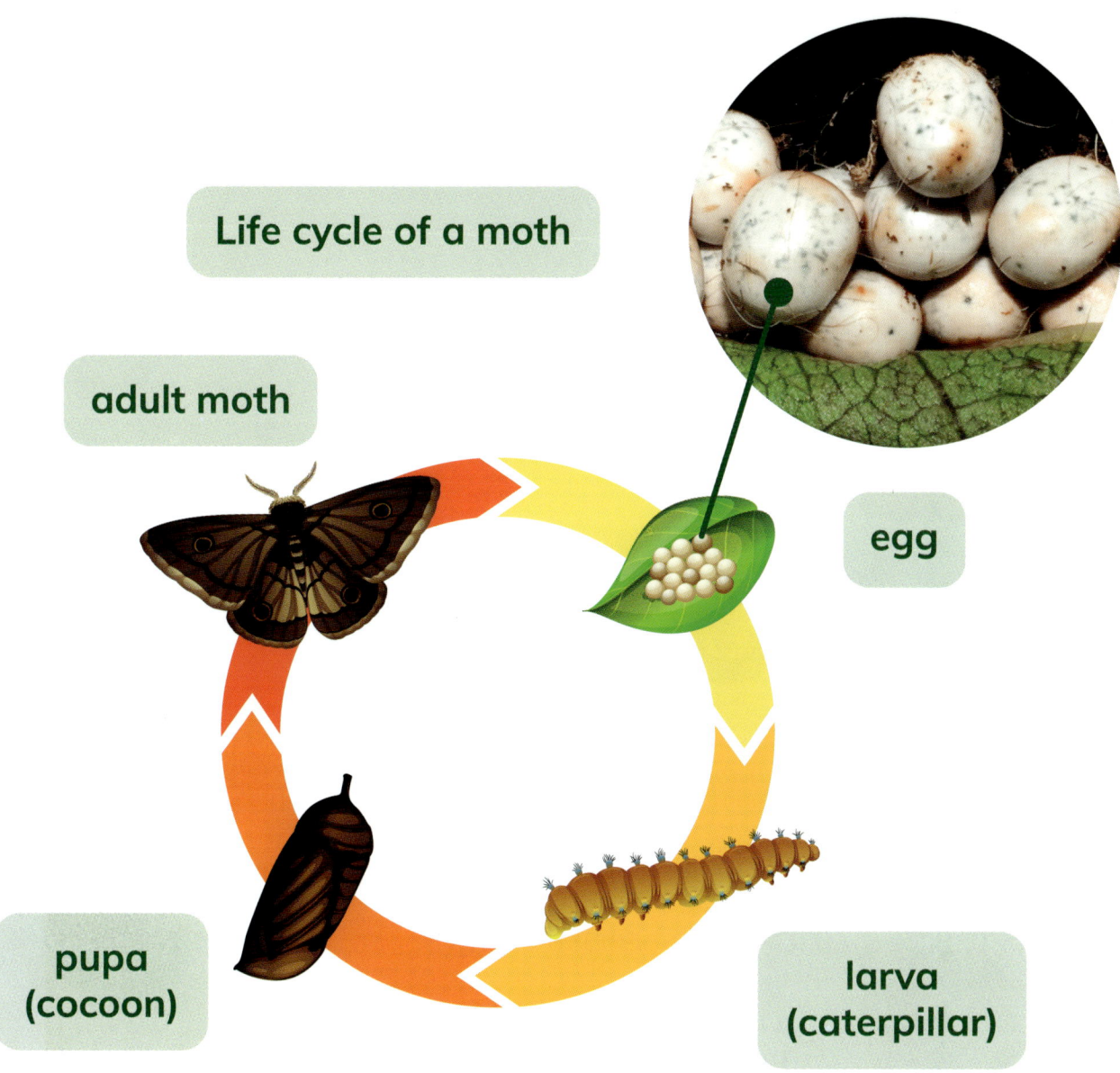

Butterflies usually lay **eggs** on plant leaves or stems. Moths lay **eggs** on tree bark, branches and leaves. Adults lay the **eggs** where the **larvae**, or caterpillars, will have food when they hatch.

EAT AND GROW

Chomp!

Caterpillars mostly chew on leaves and other plant parts. Caterpillars eat and eat. They grow and grow. A fully grown caterpillar can be more than **100 times larger** than when it first came out of the egg!

moth cocoon

Finally, the changes are done.

Split!

The **cocoon** or **chrysalis** opens. The butterfly or moth dries its wings and takes flight. **Up, up** and **away!**

NEW PLACES

See all the butterflies **flying** together?

Monarch butterflies **migrate** more than **4,800 kilometres (3,000 miles)** from the United States to Mexico and back again!

monarch butterflies

Some butterflies and moths **migrate** to escape cold weather or find food.

moth

WARMING UP

Brrr!

Thousands of monarch butterflies stick together, or **cluster,** to keep warm. Butterflies also **"sun bake"** to warm up. They lie in the Sun with their wings open.

butterfly

Do you ever **shiver** when you are cold? Both butterflies and moths can move their wings really fast to **warm up.** It looks like **shivering.**

moth

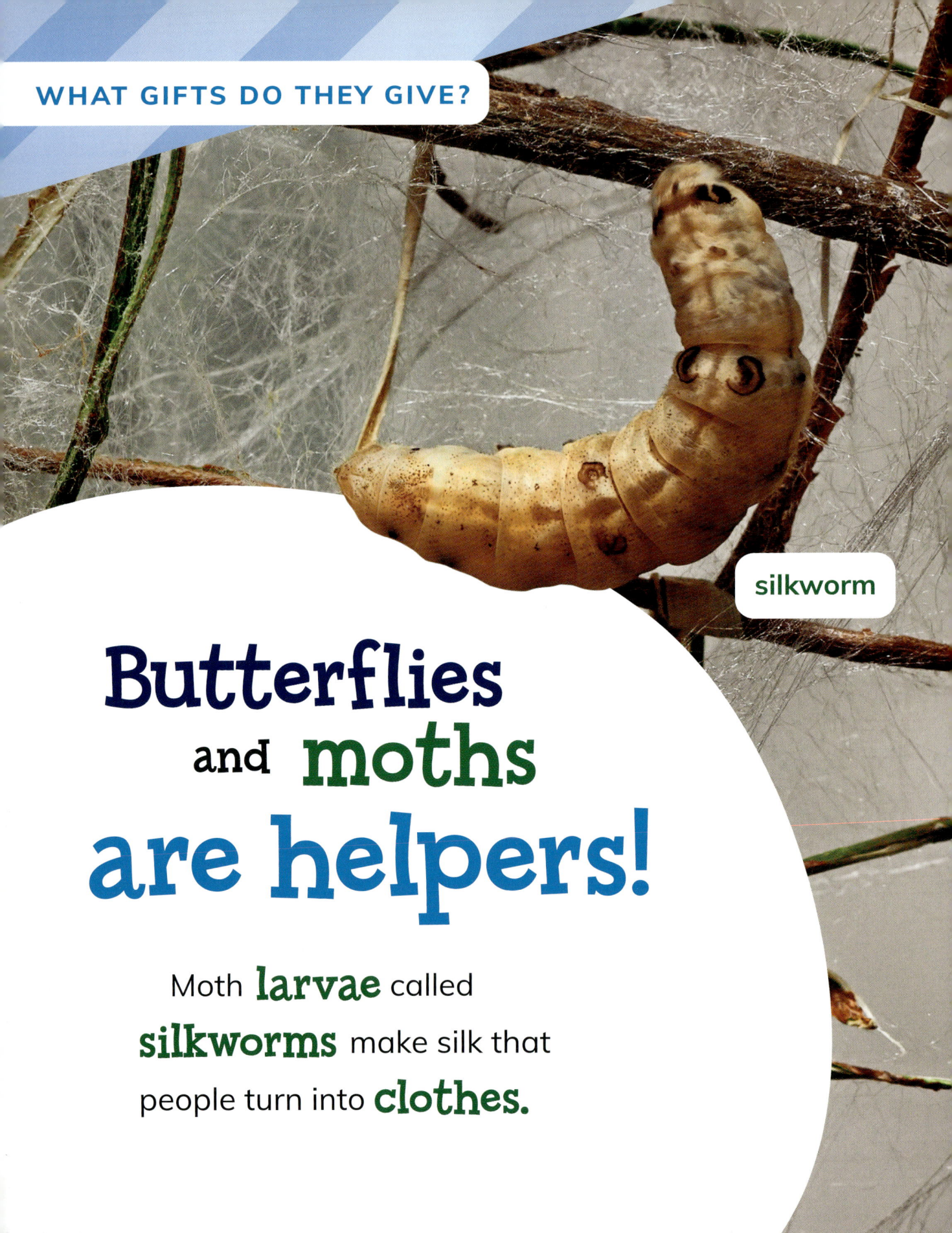

WHAT GIFTS DO THEY GIVE?

silkworm

Butterflies and moths are helpers!

Moth **larvae** called **silkworms** make silk that people turn into **clothes.**

Butterflies and moths are **pollinators.** They take pollen from plant to plant to help **new plants** grow. What's your favourite flower? You can thank **butterflies** and **moths** for the **beautiful blooms!**

butterfly

IS IT A BUTTERFLY OR A MOTH?

1. You see it fluttering at night. Is it a butterfly or a moth?

2. It landed on a flower, and its wings are closed. Is it a butterfly or a moth?

3. Its antennae are feathery and short. Is it a butterfly or a moth?

4. It is clustered together with others hanging in a tree. Is it a butterfly or a moth?

5. Its wings are brightly coloured and it has a smooth, thin body. Is it a butterfly or a moth?

Answer key: 1. moth 2. butterfly 3. moth 4. butterfly 5. butterfly